BEAUTY WILL BE CONVULSIVE

Beauty
Will Be
Convulsive

Matt Gonzalez

fmsbw

San Francisco, California

ISBN-13: 978-1-7362624-2-9

"Language and the orb-crate" appeared in *Lightning Strikes: 18 poets. 18 artists.* (San Francisco: Dolby Chadwick Gallery, 2016); "Sugar Poem" appeared in *Reverberations: A Visual Conversation* (Sebastopol: RiskPress, 2018); "Lamentations" appeared in *Lightning Strikes II: 22 poets. 22 artists.* (San Francisco: Dolby Chadwick Gallery, 2020); "Your Handwriting" and "Longer" appeared in *Stay Inspired: Shelter in Place 2020* (San Francisco: Dolby Chadwick Gallery, 2020); and "The Letter and Syllable" appeared as a broadside (San Francisco: FMSBW, 2020).

The Violet Suitcase (San Francisco: Lew Editions, 2011) is reprinted in its entirety; "Considering the Ascension of My Soul" appeared as a miniature broadside (San Francisco: Nomadic Ground, 2012).

Cover artwork by Rachel Dwan

Author photo by Michelle Fernandez

fmsbw

San Francisco, California

For Paul Grandpierre,
who I would have liked to have shared these with

& for Micah Ballard,
who first gave some of these poems a life outside of drawers
and notebooks

CONTENTS

Beauty is like a train that ceaselessly roars
out of the Gare de Lyon and which I know
will never leave, which has not left. It consists
of jolts and shocks, many of which do not
have much importance, but which we know are
destined to produce one *Shock*, which does.
Which has all the importance I do not want to
arrogate to myself. In every domain the mind
appropriates certain rights which it does not
possess. Beauty, neither static nor dynamic.
The human heart, beautiful as a seismograph...
Beauty will be CONVULSIVE or will not be at all.

André Breton, *from Nadja (1928)*
Translated by Richard Howard

BEAUTY WILL BE CONVULSIVE

2014-2020

LAMENTATION
For Paul Celan

The women whose dresses you touched
Gave you a necklace of hands
To your hair a darker blue is imparted
Blackened some, the tongue leaps, I sing
How could we have lived here?
Lamentations are at my heels like barking dogs
Chasing me across the lawn
Panting heavy like rain clouds
Threads of cloth like floss in their teeth
This is the oblivion you said I'd have someday
Your mistress turns toward the window
She will be murdered soon
Is what you say to yourself every time you see her
He sleeps through the battle and summer
I put your hair against my lips
I rub the strands of your hair against my arm
I sang it in autumn
With tulips
Whose light-shadow lifts me by the armpits
My heels have wings
Grope your way up
With our lilac voices, heaven-ravaged
It wears the white wig as I do & speaks hoarsely
Lift me by the collar of my pant legs
& release me

LANGUAGE AND THE ORB-CRATE

For Sherie' Franssen

Descending amid the living
Bearing crayons and pencils as witness
And a bowl of ceramic fruit for collateral
They walk toward the riverbank to draw
The surface clean as a sheet of paper ready to be scribbled on
I have graffiti on the walls of my lungs
Written with cigarette tar, some of it in foreign slang
Everything in nature has writing somewhere
Mark-making reliquaries speak close-mouthed
As the trees bend over the canvas like slanted parapets
A platform where an audience perches and harness a swing
Forming memory-derivations to be excavated later
And erase shadows for the present, for future-breath
We have all lived this, you and I
Because we value the things we love
Because we honor the things we were
Figures painted in tricot lingerie and blue jeans mingle with
bathers today
Fire ants run along the rocky embankment, carrying cast-away
leaves as umbrellas
Totems to ward off a phantom storm
They carry dried birch branch for scaling walls
To launch boats from the shore and carry carrion with
Today is not a day for swimming, it is a day of poems
She said You will always come back to being the way I saw you
the first time
This make-believe ambiance-cloud predominates now
There are horse races at the Heliopolis today
I want to have someone pour liquor for me all day long
Light my cigarettes and read racing forms to me
Remembering that time in Antigua I walked through streets for
coffee
Barefooted because the spider monkeys had taken my shoes
You following, laughing at me, making a chalk drawing on the
cobbled street
The sunlight makes colors disheveled you said

The rays strafing the ground where you drew on your hands and knees
When I finally spoke to you even my language was staccato
Later, we drank Chianti and I don't even like it
But I won ten thousand quetzales when Esculente won the fourth race
Everything else will follow now I said to no one in particular
The hedges I spy from are tearing my line of vision
It's blinking like a film reel
I can hear the bathers splashing water
A blessing and baptism for the red ants
Working, loafing, breathing
They run for cover just as I do

SUGAR POEM
For Adam Feibelman

On the crest of my sleeve
Fibers lift starry, wreath-like flakes
A baker's pinch
I smear it against my brow
With my wrist in haste
Now manifest as powder
For dousing pastries
Where does it come from?
Hurrying along a footpath
Blinded by glare of shimmering metal
Refracting light & dark
I see it lifted by stilts along railroad tracks
Blue fog descends like the pause before a hailstorm
The Sugar Fairy sleeps when darkness falls
Here, after riding barges to Hawaii and back
Her pillows filled with granulated or superfine
The first time I ever saw it snowing
The sky darkened with streaks of azure
Dandelions covered the ground
Made of glass or sugar, everywhere
I ran & flattened the icing under my feet
Those footprints, imparting a flavor
Are cast in memory now
Did you know rubbing sugar in wounds can heal?
There are other things I know
Men have carried it over mountain passes
Made liquor with it
Fought wars for it
Mixed it with chocolate
And put it in loaves of bread
Which I carry under my arm
Carefully with lightsoil, pitched upright
Float above my dream & cordon them
As if in conversation
There is so much, toward you
This taste

YOUR HANDWRITING

For Rachel Dwan

I held the page up close to my face
To see the groves and blemishes
Crossing paths now for a while
Like the lines of your paintings
Often repeating a rhythm
We inhabit the same neighborhood
And curated moments
Now we embrace on this folded page
The creases and ink show you've been here
I've been there too
The breathing on and handling of the paper
Without meaning to, no thought given
I keep an eye on you
So much happiness and loneliness
This life
It's hard to fathom, we do it for so often
I desire life without hurry
Calmness finds me, it could be said
Knowing you are close is enough

THE LETTER AND SYLLABLE
For Lawrence Ferlinghetti

You brought the poems to us
On your shoulder, leaning against your hip
Occasionally by the shirt collar
Or lying on their cleft-page shields
Some were lunch poems priced a penny each
Others akin to the guttural-canticles
Hearing their be-imaged voices
All the while, in your front pocket
Like a forest grass veiled from daylight
You were saving yours for later
Knowing that every reader asks to be fed impertinences
Yet no yawn exited your mouth
Janitor. Lover. Bricklayer of the word.
Priest. Cyclist. *But not jailer.*
In sense of light-splinter
With a bark-beater in each hand
You scatter-smashed the pulp to make a landing
For the sentence and paragraph
Image and copy, soul-occurred
Codices filled with mouthfuls of silent narrative
Then as now, sister to the in-mostly hurled
Some of those names didn't go away
Ashes charred and scattered, for most
The cranium-hammered
You and a couple of other kids, gray now
A life of blossom-humor
And autumn-protest, well spent
The gone world behind and in front of you
Release the glance-wind
Let your lips find the word once more
This life abhors those who squander
The letter and syllable

Written on the occasion of Lawrence's 101st birthday

LETTER
For Tamsin Smith

I meant to tell you when you were here that I saw those raccoons
trying to reach the second landing of the fire escape again, one
held back and was standing apart near where the yellow pansies
grow, along the wood fence line

He was just peering at the others, with a styrofoam cup in its paw,
doubtful of success

I neared the window, and thank god the pane didn't shatter,
because it let me get close enough to make eye contact with the
most forward one, and we had a moment of recognition

I imagine she was thankful the glass held also, though she tried to
put on an air of confidence, just as I did

The underbrush has been cleared in the yard again, all the star lilies
clustered on the slope, all the way back to the neighbor's faucet,
the one with the red wheel handle, I assume they make their way
through the gap between the fence line and the eucalyptus, which
is hard to see because of the furrows in the bark and the way the
sunlight pours between the slats of the enclosure, confusing the eye

I worry more that its branches are going to fall, like the time one of
the living room windows did shatter from the impact, do you
remember that? Or was that before I knew you?

I had a strange thought that I should tell you all of this, but after
you left, I realized I had forgotten, because it happened while you
went off to see if there were more bottles of the *Magnien*
bourgogne we like, that I should write it down so I wouldn't forget

Even though it's in my head now

But since we'll lay down together soon, you'll be in proximity to it
in any event

I think I got distracted because I had just been talking to Micah at the cafe and then I saw Lorca on Divisidero Street waiting for us, and I could see the fog rushing over West of Twin Peaks and I noticed how everything was in the shadow that was cast

I saw that broad-headed Labrador retriever, again, chewing on the bitter irises that grow in the sidewalk planters over on Grove Street, did I tell you that?

But I'm writing this now because it was you I was thinking of, all the time, even when I didn't remember to tell you the raccoons got close

Next time I shouldn't be writing you a letter because I can just tell you

You should have been here to say hello, you're more welcoming than I am, and they would have appreciated meeting you

I didn't know how lacking I was in this regard before I loved you

My head knows how empty this place is when you run off to make errands

I'm pretty sure you're coming back, your paints and brushes are here, but I worry you'll realize all my faults while you're away

You're in my head now and I'm going to learn to say the things that I mean to say

Like the way I first learned to speak a language

It's you I was thinking of when I learned the alphabet, even though I hadn't thought of you

I promise to sort it all out and not make so many allowances for myself

Although, looking out the window now, I do think the branches are going to fall again

Would you help me trim them?

GREEN WATER PISTOL
For Devin John

I wouldn't imagine you lacking confidence
Not given how many scars are involved
Traversing the expanse of vehemence
Ten thousand times in the flight-shadow
You know, those four-minute films
Only approximate what you believe in
That attenuated necklace I liked
Was a prop you liked too
That's the story of manner & perorations
Pled over a bottle of wine with resplendent drifters
The sound of bare feet striking wood floors
Incandescent bulbs flickering like fireflies
I've heard the pitter-patter
Searching for a hiding place
Where closets became a holy hermitage
Reeking of vinegar and water
Filled to the brim with wreaths to lay
I see the record player is broken
Although the radio dial is within reach
Shall we turn it on?
To conceal the silence between the words we make
Before we take things to keep them from being lost
Folding them between evocations of regrets
Carried like talismans in our front pockets
Charms we can rub when betting on horses
Or telling a stranger, cherished secrets
What difference does it make?
Because I'm always going to remember
That time you tried to cut your appendix out
Or scratched your knee playing badminton
Or straightened your hair with an iron
It's all just so ordinary
But it isn't

MEXICANS IN SPACE
For Emilio Villalba & Michelle Fernandez

Not again
Skateboarder
The smoke billowing out of windows
The park riddled with crosses and concrete
Ramps and trees
Maya astronaut
Wearing leather helmet and chinstrap
I'll carry you, if you promise to carry me
And the assessment that we
have pints of blood to spare
Electric sparks coming out of our ears
In the *Popol Vuh,* Camazotz expelled
Trying to flip his board
Let the bats be godless
The Hero Twins have to sleep somewhere
When storm clouds gather
Even birds flee
The nighttime invites us
Hiding under pool tables
On the atrium reading poetry
Dangling from ropes
Tendons in your arm are taunt
Harnessed to this world
Put your eye through the viewfinder
Let your finger pause life
Capture and archive
The moments that are too precious
To let go without a fight

JUST LIKE THAT

I saw it all in a dream before it happened
Galleons idling off the coast
Awaiting news of those first boats
There is a pendency to anxiety
Wondering how the advance party will fare
Is this the dream that's coming real?
I ask myself upon waking
Because we all know it's capable of that
The pavement littered with stencil art
From trash bins I hear running water
I scan the sky for scrub jays
Some manifestation
Like an eagle perched on a cactus
With a snake in its mouth
Don't hold your breath the passing girl
Whispered to no one except me
The streets covered with packaging
Coca-Cola red & *Modelo* blue
I can't stop to gather it all
So, I read the writing on the ground
Prefab glyphs on pavement talking aloud to me
And just like that
I'm here
Before we release ourselves and gather evidence
Let's be truthful for once
It's all a distraction from the fact we're going to die someday
And that erasure compels gesture and thought
The betrayal of living as assured as my voice
Traveling along the contours and space between us
Looking for a listener
Forlorn or not, confident or startled
I ask the woman for a cigarette knowing she didn't have one
And I don't want it anyway
Taking comfort in a stranger apologizing to me
It's why man invented smoking and the asking of directions
I rub my shoulder hesitating to venture forward
And just like that

I'm here again
There are considerations to be undertaken
How a path narrows in places less travelled
How it expands inviting rest
When I pitch my tent, I fear sloped ground
I consider how rain might gather
In puddles or fissures
I've been thinking about water my whole life
I learned to swim in the *Amniotic River*
Narrow tributary of the *Rio Grande*
Avoided being carried out to sea
I've wanted to be land-bound
A safe distance away to watch impending boats
Threatening them with my stare
Throwing shade before that was a thing
Sizing up the enemy
Before retreating into the forest of hidden thoughts
And dense bush of vocabulary
And just like that
The picnic table has a tablecloth on it
Checkered red and varieties of such
We feign a voyage in nature hostile to glass & concrete
Yet pick up a plastic fork and imagine *primitive*
André Breton cleaned his feet
On books he didn't like
Henry Thoreau was jailed for not paying taxes
Which one more honorable?
And standing some distance away
A kind of dice throwing
The boat bobbing on the coast
Portending change
And just like that
I'm here

LONGER

I saw a blue jay in the buckeye tree this morning
He was singing to another bird and
Prancing on various branches
As he spoke his language
There was condensation on the ground
As I walked out of my apartment
Water has a way of cleaning everything
And making it shiny
The clouds were expanding and tumbling
As if they were wrestlers grappling on the ground
Breathing heavy
A passerby filled with apprehension
Asked me if I had seen her terrier
He must have gotten off of his leash
I imagined he was happily running
On the north side of the park with other dogs
I could see his tongue hanging out of his mouth
As he scurried up the embankment
That's how I feel standing here
Taking stock of my surroundings
Breathing deeply
Running my hand through my hair
With no place I need to be
And no errand that can't wait till later
Sometimes it's like that
We pause to take a moment
And see ourselves from above
The gratitude I have for all of my troubles
How lucky I have been
Whether strife or generosity
To have anything
I hope I get to do this longer

MY FATHER & ERIC'S POEM

For Éric Antoine

All on your mail is new to me
the movement must have been very small
I have no one to ask
but I will look more into it
more thoroughly
I lived quite some unfair moments lately
but you are here, and this is all I think about.
Spring and my work also save me
I try to focus on the good things
The things that are growing still
Recalling the hustle and bustle of adolescence
And I have your white collage
That reminds me of good times,
every day at breakfast!
I see the painting you made me
I'm ok.

POEM TO GIRLS

For Jenny Monick

Conversation oscillating
Amidst random & highly contoured angles
Your uncertainty, yet still-confined
Pulled together by certain consistencies
Delicacy of touch & intimacy of scale
Preoccupied with your hands, especially
As both a subject and art-making tool
You present a ghostly intimation for me
Following me for years
Faded cloth & strands of hair
Lurking around corners
Contours of the imagination considered
Sprinkled with lavender oil
The drawings you made rubbing sheets of paper
On the floor with your arm
The smudges & stains, holes even
Tell me who you are
The losses and everything suffered
The oaths that you have taken
Resting on a mirror, your elbow, a testament
I fear that you are excessively something
I don't have words for
I can see that you are lacking modesty
And yet, you cover your body
As if it were the 19th century
When one takes into account all that has
Preceded gas lamp posts
On the edge of the foliage filled park
The strand of emotion sewn together
When you first didn't look toward me
After watching *Fitzcarraldo*
At the theatre on Broadway
The related ideas that hovered between us
Even then
Memorable in your quietness
Bundled in your winter coat

Threads interlocking with mine
How little we spoke
In the presence of ourselves
Later, riding lakes together
Our reflections casting eyes at us carefully
Our sleeping bags tossed side by side
We carried our canoe over rugged terrain
Hardly can we call them trails
I spotted you so that you could catch your breath
All of it into my face
As we rested, carrying double packs
Covered in mud & sweat
Crouched in darkness, by campfire
Fish bones held delicately in our fingers
Passed back and forth
Handled like a last cigarette, shared
The harnessing of silence
Casting abject shadows toward me
Waiting for black bears to come closer
Oblivious to all else
How many years later
Our rendezvous at the children's playground
Where I didn't look at you from a distance
Hidden behind a curtain of prohibitions
Though it was tired daylight
Eyes talking to one another, yet fleeting
As if spies in some performance
I should have walked towards you for an embrace
Coming to terms knowing
I might never see you again
I dedicate this poem to girls
A word which you hate me using

THE GATHERING

Perfume made of Summer smell

Hovers over the field

The Bathers in repose

They are all sovereign

To rule the riverbank & taunt water

No enmity in sand

Gaiety gushing & foaming

No fish blemish calm waters

I am weary and lie in solace, *just idle*

My makeshift lair cushioned by leaves

The riverbank is for contemplation

But here now, comes disruption

The bathers gather & disrobe

Their bodies cascading into water

While the day rests in capitulated light

A young woman barely clothed

Water dripping from her limbs

Steps delicately toward me

Testing each step as if the ground might collapse

I can see her bare feet

The reflection off the sunglasses nestled in her hair

Like a searchlight

A beacon to rescue

Or instrument to capture fugitives

I hold my breath, there is no sorrow left to memory

Whether blurred or excited

The lens of pleasure watching others

Is turned toward me

Finally, her glance put an arm around me

GALLOPING

All of this happened in fragments
While I was sleeping
The story I saw was like a myth
Asking me to peer through a catalog of images
Searching for the cadence & suspense
Like rain covered windows
I was rooting for the leading man, a hero
His visage, intuitive
Sharp angled & blemished
With dreams filled with labors to complete
Sounds in my head over the loudspeaker
Cautioning me about this & that
I wish I had ignored it & worn armor
Sensing the indignity that was coming
I turned away, not wanting this to end
Like the Mexican Revolution
All my favorites shot dead
My wooden horses are saddled
Ready to gallop wherever it must be
Touching shoulders from time to time
Anticipating departure, they sleep standing
The ink comes off in my hand
In the dark it resembles blood or chocolate
I see the trough and dimples
Like ravines to hide in
The glue-smears & paper-rash
As I pulled open the flap
Where the dream's tongue touched adhesive
Filled with entreaties
The canopy made of clouds levitates above me
Like a kite that's found its hitch
Jacob is wrestling with an angel
He's going to tag me any moment now
Before daybreak
This too shall be recorded
On the LP of my life
Attestation written with yawning channels

All of it halting & convulsive
Knowing that I must sharpen a blade
& wield an axe
To make this movie my own

CREST-FALLEN
For Robert Dunlap

Crest-fallen, frostbitten
Wheelbarrow made of wood
Filled with leaves pulled
From trees before they
Were ready to fall
You rake memories
From the knotted bark-covered limbs
As if bagging raindrops
Dreaming of sunlight
Reckonings happen
In moments like this
One eye on the mirage of repose
Glass tears under your other
I don't have to tell you
How this life is
Sometimes not given a chance
To fall onto the ground
In our own time

RIB CAGE BE STRONG

For Tamsin Smith

Rib cage be strong on this lithe body
Protect it from adversaries and mishaps
Surround her heart carefully
Tighten the space between bones
Lest any foreign object pierce her

Cover me with her smell
So I may breathe it freely
Put it in my hair and on my fingers
Against my torso, on my cheeks

I chew her hair in the dark
Inhale her exhale with pleasure
Weigh her down with a heavier mass
Made lighter by the promise of tomorrow

My rule for you is simple, so listen
No leaving

THE VIOLET SUITCASE

1992-2004

WEST OF MANHATTAN

For Jack Micheline

White hair and scarlet lap
Indian yellow here and there
Hunter and quarry
Stilled in a drama
Dissolve in hailstorms
Broken seas

Rapture of charms
Correct impenitent vices
He sleeps in sailor's garb today
With ragged and wrinkled bellies
Among clouds, lateness comes
Perishable caress

He is related to Elizabethans
Whatever the hell that means
And tightens his chinstrap
Balloon-footed, whistling
A monarchy, whore, and rockabye

In dull disdain
Haunting his city
Spawning wings
Just want to get drunk and sing songs

WHERE

For Sarah Berger

Yet they revealed
Nothing
To one another
When they spoke
Apparently in the middle
Of something
A clearing, under olive trees
Using for molds such
Ordinary objects as a hand & mouth
Dispatched & enduring
Even impressions discussed
Kind of, or –
Melodramas in the provincial
With incessant teasing
& quaint reminders
Of the neighborhood theater
Now, where to go
I have to ask you
Out toward vastness
Or toward soul?

SAINT SANG
For Felix Macnee

Enveloped in a wave of black
Cages stuffed with ladders
Ridiculed, then devoured by balconies
While people were forgetting their affairs
Four sirens held in my hand
& white starched streamers hanging
From the City of Liquors
And the snarling stars look toward me
As I make my way toward my home
Then I heard
Boom

SONG

For Tadeusz Borowski

A burned-out forest, cream-colored now
Made of jewels & scorched tiles
The left-over trees stand crooked
Briefly, see them perishing

Scatter this thought out of your head
Trade bootleg whiskey for cashmere lingerie
Tantalizing isn't it?
But this is not your last home

And what do you have? Some fragile songs
Suffering somewhere & barbed wire
And it freezes
Now it freezes

Parade music & geraniums hang into your window
A nest of spiders, they are barefooted now
All along the ramparts, austere like
& scatter this song

CONSIDERING THE ASCENSION OF MY SOUL

Looking for my handkerchief
Thrice died
First by Dada
Then by Surrealism
Then by Marxism
I wonder if there is space on the carousel
I am being consumed by intellectuality
Need magic incantation
I'll make the sign of the cross
Then die of laughter

THROUGH CUBIST LANDSCAPES
For Catherine Rauschuber

Good to see trees, sometimes
In landscapes blurred as if painted
By Cézanne
Fore surely they would know
To tell me something – if necessary
Dull browns & dark blues
Are my favorites
With a dash of yellow – dull yellow
Mustard like
& I am certain that I haven't fallen lost yet
Though fleeing sometimes
In dreams I stumble – awkwardly
Always through cubist landscapes – barely
Catching a train – & being crestfallen
& burdenheavy with my departure
Because I can't evoke the things I need
But now – not pursued but clear-headed
Poignant & sound of mind
Remembering how I was
Accosted by you the other night
Well, I can't very well forget
Your breath & all
So, I declare
Roger Fry is the only painter
& how many more nights do I look forward to?
Thousands, & then some

ONLY TRAINS
For Blaise Cendrars

From the galleries and upheavals of 1912
You rode straddling centuries
With no bloody flowers or tartar cakes
You rode

From the rundown circuses
Octopuses stood you up
How many kitchens did you see
How many Eiffel towers, how many precipices

From Carthage to the edge of the Ganges
The skies are mad sometimes
They dazzle you, cluttered with zeppelins
And one thousand newspapers

You threw your arm away at Champagne
And drinking sometimes you wore dresses
Butterflies the size of your hand
Soaking in castor oil

And Caruso singing in an old movie house
Pure marvels and smoked eel
They are all cinders now
Inimitable and dear

Comforting to witness this academy
Floating in the current
Under constellations and a smashed heart
Made hollow by your bare hand

Capricious eye and drowning gills
Crowding songs and a charcoal liturgy
It has come to this
Only this

I see only trains

VIRGIL

For Michael Jones

Eyes lively beauty
Brave in heart
Terrify me
Double dress shoulders
His mind with her words
I wait for prizes

Humbly supplicate Italian cities
Retreating
With rocks and a whirling pool
Winter however long
Uninterrupted discourse
Nevertheless arousing

Wretched Greeks
Carry off plunder
With no distinction
You shall have these arms
Bloody, waving a club, heavy with knots

What is the cause of your march?
Though beautiful in arms
You stand in the shallows
Rage the more increases
Arrows being thrown
Send forth now a foaming wave of blood

CLOSER

She turned the
corner wearing
her red ski cap and
I whispered closer closer

She asked me what
I wanted and
I was pretty much
horrorstricken

Before I could
explain myself
she touched the
lapel of my coat

Just then
I noticed three
boys dragging a
piece of driftwood
across the street
and I had an impulse
to go help them

There now I
said to her –
You get a laurel
wreath for your head

She laughed aloud

BENEDICTION
For Micah Ballard

When I spoke to you
Leaves were coming out of your mouth
I commented on how blond your hair was
& you said perhaps
Later you asked me if my coat was heavy
& I was furious on all accounts
All the thoughts in my head came running
Down Fillmore street overtaking the buses
& skateboarders & many glorious recollections
Of days past poured forth
& I averted my gaze from yours
To hide my soul & now thinking about it
I am laaaughing so loud my friends
Can hear it through the other side of the door
So before you prop yourself up
& peer at me know that this
Is my benediction for you.

Matt Gonzalez, 2017

Matt Gonzalez was born in McAllen, Texas, and received a BA from Columbia University in New York City. He has lived in San Francisco since 1991, working both as a public defender and in private practice, handling civil rights cases. In 2011, poet Micah Ballard's imprint Lew Editions published *The Violet Suitcase,* a collection of ten of Gonzalez's poems written between 1992 and 2004.

In addition to writing poetry, Gonzalez is a visual artist working in the medium of found paper collage. His first solo exhibition was at Adobe Books Backroom Gallery in 2007, and he has also had one-person shows at Park Life (San Francisco); In vitro Gallery (Chicago); and Dolby Chadwick Gallery (San Francisco), where he has been exhibiting since 2014.

THE PAGE POETS SERIES

www.ingramcontent.com/pod-product-compliance
Lightning Source LLC
Chambersburg PA
CBHW032104040426
42449CB00007B/1181